A Taste of Greece!

Recipes by "Rena tis Ftelias"
Rena's collection of the best Greek,
Mediterranean recipes!

EIRINI TOGIA

English edition
Copyright by Eirini Togia - All rights reserved - 2014

Written and cooked by
Eirini Togia

Photos by
Vangelis Paterakis

Direction and food styling by
Konstantinos Togias

Gourmets
Bessy Togia, Gina Togia

Translated into English and edited by
Vasileios Tziovaras

Proofreader
Kayleigh Hames

Copyright

A taste of Greece! Recipes by "Rena tis Ftelias": Rena's collection of the best Greek, Mediterranean recipes!

Greek title: Rena Tis Ftelias: Dishes we have loved!
Parent ISBN: 978-1-910370-08-7

Authored by © Eirini Togia, 2014
Photos by © Vangelis Paterakis
Photo stock agency: Dreamstime.com

English - print edition
ISBN: 978-1-910370-04-9
(Paperback, Stergiou Limited)
ISBN: 978-1-910370-53-7
(Hardcover, Stergiou Limited)
ISBN: 978-1500939403
(Paperback, CreateSpace)

English - digital edition
ISBN-EPUB: 978-1-910370-05-6
ISBN-MOBI: 978-1-910370-06-3
ISBN-PDF: 978-1-910370-07-0

Published by Stergiou Limited
Distribution: Worldwide, exclusive

STERGIOU LIMITED
Publications & Media Services
Suite A, 6 Honduras Street, London
EC1Y 0TH, United Kingdom
Tel.: +44 (0) 20 7504 1325
Fax: +44 (0) 20 76920609
Email: publications@stergioultd.com
Web: http://stergioultd.com

To my family
and the people
I love!

SPECIAL THANKS
Many thanks to **Sarris' catering**, and especially to Mr. **Manolis Pangalos** for his supply of the tableware used for the photography.

Contents

Introduction 7

My childhood's gemista (stuffed peppers and tomatoes)! 8

Salad with black-eyed beans, flavouring & olives 10

Crispy domatokeftedes (tomato fritters) with lots of peppermint 12

Aromatic hortopita (vegetable and cheese pie) with homemade filo (dough) 14

Octopus salad with multi-coloured peppers and lots of flavouring 16

Stuffed squids 18

Colourful salad with potatoes and courgettes 20

Fried eggs and tomatoes 22

Crispy kadaifi pastry stuffed with a variety of Greek cheeses 24

Stuffed beets with yoghurt and grated walnuts 26

Shrimps saganaki with fresh tomatoes, feta cheese and ouzo 28

Rena's pâté with Greek smoked salmon 30

Vegetable garden... cooked in the oven 32

Dolmades (stuffed grape leaves) with fresh leaves! 34

Bean stew with potatoes 36

Sofrito (pan-fried veal with potatoes): the original recipe from Corfu! 38

Chicken stew with okra 40

Stuffed aubergines (imam bayildi) 42

Hearty fasolada (bean soup) with plenty of celery and sweet Florina peppers! 44

Stuffed courgettes with minced beef and avgolemono (egg-lemon sauce) 46

The traditional pastitsada... with cinnamon flavour 48

Stuffed meatloaves with omelette and graviera 50

Bite-sized pieces of veal cooked in the pot with feta cheese and Kalamata olives 52

Artichokes with peas, potatoes and lots of lemon 54

Braised chicken with chilopites (Greek noodles) 56

The famous oven-baked lamb with lemon and oregano 58

Giouvetsi cooked in the pot (veal stew) 60

Cod bites with skordalia (garlic dip) 62

Perch bianco (white) stew with lemon juice and potatoes 64

Our grandmother's giouvarlakia (meatball soup) 66

Pork stew with leeks and celery... no further comment necessary 68

Stuffed aubergines with feta sauce 70

Cuttlefish stew with flavouring and orzo 72

Crispy, pan-fried meatballs 74

Cauliflower yiahni (stew) 76

Oven-baked aromatic butter beans with herbs 78

The classic moussaka; aromatic and light 80

Chicken bites with dill and courgettes 82

Pork stew with beans 84

Shrimp salad with rice; full of colours and aromatic! 86

Bouillabaisse... fish soup 88

Loukoumades with yoghurt 90

Samali (semolina cake with syrup) 92

Homemade jam of 3 kinds of peaches 94

Vissinada (cherry juice): offer it to your guests! 96

Chef Eirini Togia 98

© Anna Raspopova | Dreamstime.com

Introduction

35 full years have passed and we haven't even realised it! Together we've travelled from Mykonos to Athens and wherever else our taste memories led us. Together we've remembered our childhood flavours, and together we've discovered and fell in love with new ones through simple and traditional recipes. I have wanted for a long time to share some of the best recipes of all these years with you. So here I am now, ready to make this happen! And, by the way, I would like to thank you all for those moments we've shared together throughout these years.

This is not where inspiration and creations stop. To be continued...

My childhood's gemista (stuffed peppers and tomatoes)!

It's a recipe every household used to prepare, especially in the summer, as this dish's ingredients are seasonal to summer after all. We enjoy it with a slice of feta cheese and some bread.

Serves ● ● ● ● ● ● 80′

Method

Preheat the oven to 200 degrees.

Slice off the top of the tomatoes, scoop out their pulp with a spoon, put some sugar inside and turn them upside down. Slice off the tops of the peppers, discard the seeds and make small cuts in 2-3 places of each pepper. Scoop out the pulp of the aubergines and cut them as you did with the peppers. Do the same with the courgettes.

In a saucepan, put the onions, half the oil, the pulp of the courgettes, the diced aubergine (all chopped in small cubes), parsley, peppermint, half the tomato juice, salt and pepper. Sauté for 2-3 minutes, add some water and, when boiling, add the rice and stir to prevent sticking together. Remove from the heat and let the filling cool slightly.

Once it has cooled a little, start filling the tomatoes, peppers, aubergines and courgettes with it one by one. Cover the tomatoes and peppers with their tops. Put them all into a baking dish. Season the potatoes with salt and pepper and spread them among the gemista.

Dress the gemista with the remaining oil, the tomatoes' flesh that was scooped out earlier in chunks, the rest of the tomato juice and the water. Cover the baking dish with aluminium foil and put it in the oven for 40-45 minutes. Remove the foil from the baking dish and leave the food in the oven for about 15 minutes, until it gets a bit of colour.

Secret

Don't boil the rice much because it will boil in the oven anyway.

Ingredients

4 mid-sized tomatoes,

3 mid-sized green peppers,

3 mid-sized aubergines,

3 mid-sized courgettes,

1kg quartered potatoes,

500g round grain rice (such as risotto or paella rice),

4 grated onions,

1 bunch of chopped parsley,

1 bunch of chopped peppermint,

1 water glass of tomato juice,

1 water glass of olive oil,

salt, pepper, sugar,

1 wine glass of tomato juice,

2 glasses of water

Salad with black-eyed beans, flavouring & olives

A simple, aromatic salad with Mykonian beans. That's right, Mykonos! That's where we tasted it for the first time! It's filling, nutritious and a great choice as a main course for someone conscious of their diet.

Serves ●●●●●●● 25'

Method

Wash the beans thoroughly.

In a pot, add plenty of water and let it boil. Once it starts boiling, add the beans and let them boil well. Strain them, rinse thoroughly to remove their blackness and let them drain and cool.

Put the beans into a salad bowl and add all the onions, parsley, dill, peppers and tomatoes. Add salt and stir all the ingredients together.

Cover the bowl with cling film and put it in the fridge for an hour or two to cool.

Shake oil and vinegar vigorously together in a shaker and dress the salad with it.

Add a little salt and pepper, the olives and serve the salad cold.

Ingredients

500g black-eyed beans (dried, not tined),

3 finely chopped onions,

1 bunch of finely chopped spring onions,

1 bunch of chopped parsley,

1 bunch of chopped dill,

4 finely chopped multi-coloured peppers,

5-6 diced juicy tomatoes,

oil, vinegar, salt and a little pepper,

Kalamata olives

© Zts | Dreamstime.com

Crispy domatokeftedes (tomato fritters) with lots of peppermint

An original, traditional recipe from Santorini. This is a quick and delicious snack accompanying ouzo, beer and white wine.

© Vangelis Paterakis

Serves ● ● ● ● 25'

Method

In a mixing bowl, stir the flour and water together thoroughly (take care of any remaining lumps).

Add the tomatoes, onions and peppermint and stir well.

Pour the oil into the pan and, when hot, add the mixture spoon by spoon and fry on both sides.

Fry the tomato fritters carefully to avoid burning them and, every time you turn them over, take care not to make any holes as these let oil into them.

There you go! Domatokeftedes with a nice reddish-beige colour.

Secrets

1. If the mixture is not thick enough, add a little more flour.
2. If you want, you can add a courgette and an aubergine, cut into small cubes.

Ingredients

4-5 diced juicy tomatoes,

2 diced onions,

1 bunch of fresh chopped peppermint,

1 teacup of water,

2 teacups of plain flour,

salt, pepper and oil for the pan

Aromatic hortopita (vegetable and cheese pie) with homemade filo (dough)

Besides a gold award, it has also won a place in our hearts! A classic pie, salty to just the right degree and aromatic to your liking. Add herbs of your choice and you will get delicious variations.

© Vangelis Paterakis

Makes   1 baking dish   45'

Method

Prepare the filo dough. In a mixing bowl, mix and knead the ingredients thoroughly until you form a homogeneous dough. Separate the dough into two halves.

Preheat the oven to 160 degrees.

Remove the roots and discard the yellow leaves from the spinach then rinse it well. Let it drain. In a pot over low heat, add the oil along with all the onions, leeks, dill, salt and pepper and let them boil for about 10 minutes to wilt them down. Add the well-drained spinach and leave the pot on the heat until the spinach reabsorbs its juices. Remove from the heat and let the mixture cool.

Add the eggs, feta cheese, grated Cheddar cheese and milk to the mixture. Mix all the ingredients with your hands thoroughly until they become a homogeneous mixture.

Separate the dough into two equal pieces and use a rolling pin to spread each filo into a thin layer. Make two filos. Spread a little oil in a baking dish, lay one filo and add the mixture. Lay the second filo over the mixture and add a little oil on top. Cut the hortopita into pieces.

Put the baking dish into the oven and cook for about an hour.

Ingredients

For the filling

1.5kg fresh chopped spinach,

1kg leeks cut into rings,

2 grated onions,

1 bunch of finely chopped spring onions,

1 bunch of finely chopped dill,

6 eggs,

400g feta cheese cut into chunks,

200g grated Cheddar cheese,

1 wine glass of olive oil,

1 wine glass of undiluted evaporated milk,

salt and pepper,

a little oil for the baking dish

Ingredients for the filo dough

1 packet self raising flour (500g), 1 egg, 1 cup of yoghurt (200g), 1 teacup of olive oil, a little salt, 100g grated mature cheese.

Octopus salad with multi-coloured peppers and lots of flavouring

A glass of ouzo accompanied by an octopus salad... is there a better combination?

Serves ● ● ● ●

 30'

Method

Wash the octopus thoroughly with plenty of water. Put it into a pot over low heat for about 3-4 minutes. Add the wine, a little water and let it boil. When it boils, remove it from the pot and cut it into pieces.

In a large salad bowl, combine the octopus, onions, peppers, fennel and celery. Add a little salt. Cover the bowl with cling film and put in the refrigerator for 2 hours.

Shake oil and vinegar vigorously together in a shaker and dress the salad.

Serve with freshly ground pepper and a few olives.

Ingredients

1 octopus about 1000-1200g,

1 water glass of red wine,

2 onions cut into rings,

1 green pepper cut into rings,

1 red Florina pepper cut into rings,

half a bunch of finely chopped fennel,

half a bunch of finely chopped celery,

1.5 water glass of olive oil,

half a water glass of vinegar,

salt, freshly ground pepper,

a few olives for the garnish

© Alexander Raths | Dreamstime.com

Stuffed squids

Squids in cooked in an alternative fashion. Winey, light and... fantastic!

Serves ● ● ● ●  60'

Method

Wash the squids thoroughly with plenty of water.

Slice off their tentacles and clean their insides.

Remove the bone, ink, intestines and, finally, the skin.

Discard the eyes and mouth, wash the tentacles and finely cut them.

Pour 1 wine glass of oil into a pot and sauté all the onions together for 6-8 minutes.

Next, add the tentacles and deglaze with wine.

Add salt, pepper and 1 glass of water.

When the water starts to boil, add the rice and stir to prevent sticking together.

Once the rice is almost prepared, add the orange flesh, raisins and peppermint and let the mixture reabsorb its juices.

Let the filling cool, fill the squids one by one and put toothpicks through their tops to keep their filling from falling apart.

Place them again into the pot along with the 2 tablespoons of olive oil, a little water and the lemon juice.

Leave the food to simmer over a low heat and, when ready, put it on a platter and serve.

Secret

The food should simmer until the squids are soft and tender.

Ingredients

1kg mid-sized squids,

1 teacup of round grain rice (for example, paella or risotto rice),

1 wine glass of olive oil,

2-3 grated onions,

1 bunch of finely chopped spring onions,

150g raisins soaked in water for ten minutes and strained,

the diced flesh of 2 oranges,

1 bunch of finely chopped peppermint,

1 wine glass white wine,

1 wine glass lemon juice,

2 tbsp olive oil,

salt, freshly ground pepper

Colourful salad with potatoes and courgettes

For some, it's the ultimate summer salad. But surely it is the best choice for the Easter table, together with the eggs we have cracked.

Serves ●●●●●● 40′

Method

Wash the potatoes and courgettes thoroughly and boil.

Strain them and peel the potatoes while still hot. Let them cool.

In a large salad bowl, combine the potatoes, courgettes, radishes, cherry tomatoes, all the onions, parsley and dill.

Cover the bowl with cling film and put it in the fridge to cool.

Shake oil and vinegar vigorously together in a shaker along with salt, pepper and oregano.

Add the olives and eggs and dress the salad with the mixture.

Add a little bit of freshly ground pepper and serve the salad cold.

Ingredients

10 small round potatoes,

10 small courgettes,

2 quartered boiled eggs,

10 small radishes,

10 cherry tomatoes,

10-15 olives,

3-4 finely chopped spring onions,

1 bunch of finely chopped parsley,

1 bunch of finely chopped dill,

1 water glass of olive oil,

half a wine glass of vinegar,

oregano,

salt and pepper

© Cristina Annibali | Dreamstime.com

Fried eggs and tomatoes

An alternative of the famous strapatsada that is made in Corfu. You can try it for breakfast too!

Serves ● ●

 20′

Method

Put the chopped tomatoes along with the tomato juice in a pan.

Leave on low heat and, when the sauce starts to thicken, add the oil and the green pepper.

Stir the sauce and add the eggs (whole, not scrambled as in omelette).

Add salt and pepper and let the eggs cook on low heat.

Take the pan off the heat, scatter over the feta chunks and carefully shake the pan 2-3 times.

Serve it with the eggs hot.

Ingredients

4 eggs,

4-5 tomatoes peeled and cut into chunks,

1 wine glass of tomato juice,

1 finely chopped green pepper,

200g feta cheese cut into chunks,

half a wine glass of olive oil,

salt and pepper

© Shane White | Dreamstime.com

Crispy kadaifi pastry stuffed with a variety of Greek cheeses

The savoury kadaifi! An out-of-the-ordinary pie for those who love every single version of kadaifi.

Makes   20 small kadaifi pies   30'

Method

Take the pastry out of the fridge to thaw completely.

Preheat the oven to 160 degrees.

In a mixing bowl, mix the cheeses, one egg and a little less than half the cream.

Sprinkle in a little pepper and mix well.

Unroll the kadaifi and spread it, tearing apart the shreds and gently spreading them out. Take the pastry little by little, lay it and place a spoonful of the mixture on it.

Wrap each pie like a little roll folding the sides inward.

Put all the pies in a baking dish, one next to another.

In another bowl, mix the other egg with the remaining cream.

Drizzle the rolls with cream and put in the oven for about 25 minutes. Once they have a nice golden colour, they are ready.

Eat them while still hot.

Ingredients

500g kadaifi pastry,

800g grated cheeses (feta, kasseri and graviera),

2 eggs,

500g cream,

freshly ground pepper

Stuffed beets with yoghurt and grated walnuts

A different way to enjoy beets. Yoghurt takes them to a whole new level!

Serves ● ● ● ●

 40'

Method

Place a pot with plenty of water on high heat and, when it starts to boil, add the beetroots and let them boil.

Once boiled, strain and leave them cool.

Next, peel them, slice off their tops as you do with tomatoes when you want to fill them, scoop out their flesh, pour a little bit of vinegar inside and turn upside down.

In a mixing bowl, finely cut the flesh of the beetroots and add half the walnuts, vinegar, tuna, half the yoghurt, half the mayonnaise, the green apple, salt and pepper.

Stir all ingredients together and fill the beetroots one by one with the mixture.

Stir the remaining mayonnaise with the yoghurt.

Top each beetroot with a teaspoon of the yoghurt/mayonnaise mixture and some walnuts.

Cover the beetroots with cling film and put them in the refrigerator for 2 hours.

Eat them cold.

This is a very tasty and fresh salad!

Secrets

1. If you want, add a little bit of finely chopped garlic as well.
2. We boil the beetroots until soft and tender.

Ingredients

8 mid-sized beetroots,

vinegar for the beetroots,

200gr yoghurt yoghurt,

2 cups mayonnaise,

2 cups coarsely chopped walnuts,

1 wine glass of vinegar,

1 can of tuna in water, well strained and cut into chunks,

1 diced green apple,

salt and pepper

Shrimps saganaki with fresh tomatoes, feta cheese and ouzo

Classic saganaki with shrimps. With the ouzo added into the pot and the feta accompanying the shrimps, this is one of the best heady, summer dishes.

Serves ●●●● 40'

Method

Place a pot with plenty of water and the bay leaves on high heat.

Once the water starts to boil, add the shrimps and let them boil for 5-6 minutes. Strain and, once they have cooled, remove their shells.

With a sharp knife, cut a slit along their backs and remove the veins.

In a pot over medium heat, add the tomatoes along with the oil, salt, pepper, sugar and Tabasco sauce.

Add 1 wine glass of water, stir and let the sauce boil and thicken.

Shortly before removing the pot from the heat, pour the ouzo, add the shrimps and the feta and let them boil for 1-2 minutes.

Sprinkle with plenty of freshly ground pepper and serve.

Secret

When adding the shrimps, the sauce has to be already quite thick. If you want, add a little bit of finely chopped garlic as well.

Ingredients

1kg mid-sized shrimps,

3-4 bay leaves,

4-5 tomatoes peeled and cut into chunks,

1 wine glass of olive oil,

salt and freshly ground pepper,

a little sugar,

a little bit of Tabasco sauce,

1 wine glass of ouzo,

250-300g feta cheese cut into chunks

Rena's pâté with Greek smoked salmon

We wed trout with salmon, making a unique dish for our formal meals, easily and quickly.

Serves ●●●●●●●●●●   20′

Method

Clean the trout, remove their bones (if any) and put them in the blender along with the salmon, lemon juice and lemon zest. Blend for 2-3 minutes.

Put the mixture into a large bowl, add pepper, onions and mayonnaise and mix the ingredients very well.

Pour the mixture into an oblong shape, cover it with cling film and put it in the freezer for about 2 hours.

Take it out of the freezer and leave it out for 10 minutes.

Cut the pâté into pieces and wrap a salmon slice around each and every one of them.

Alternatively, place a folded salmon slice over each piece.

Serve with a little bit of finely chopped dill.

Ingredients

3 smoked trout fillets,

500g smoked salmon,

1 bunch of finely chopped spring onions,

8-10 ground black peppercorns,

3 teacups of mayonnaise,

zest of one lemon,

1 wine glass of lemon juice,

salmon slices and finely chopped dill for the garnish

© Piyato | Dreamstime.com

Vegetable garden... cooked in the oven

...known as briam or tourlou. Here's another delicious - quick and cost-effective - traditional dish. You can add whatever vegetables you have.

Serves ● ● ● ● ● ● 20'

Method

Preheat the oven to 200 degrees.

Put all of the ingredients into a baking dish and mix thoroughly. Add the water.

Cover the baking dish with aluminium foil and put it in the oven.

After about an hour, take a look at the food to see if it has cooked and reabsorbed its juices. If it needs more time, put it back into the oven and add a little more water.

Once ready, remove the foil and leave the food in the oven for about 15 minutes to get a bit of colour and for the potatoes to get roasted.

Secrets

1. Try cooking the food in a pot!
2. The ingredients aubergines, courgettes and peppers are cut in slices.

Ingredients

1kg potatoes peeled and cut into slices,

2 aubergines cut into slices,

2 courgettes cut into slices,

2 onions cut into rings,

1 green pepper cut into slices,

1 Florina pepper cut into slices,

2kg tomatoes peeled and cut into chunks,

10 okra,

10 green beans,

half a bunch of finely chopped fresh peppermint,

half a bunch of finely chopped parsley,

half a bunch of finely chopped celery,

1 wine glass of olive oil,

oregano, salt, pepper,

1 tablespoon sugar,

2 water glasses of water

Dolmades (stuffed grape leaves) with fresh leaves!

The recipe our grandmothers used to cook. Try making your own dolmades and their taste is sure to reward you!

Makes   50-60 dolmades   60'

Method

Place a pot with plenty of water over high heat and, when the water starts to boil, add the grape leaves ten by ten and cook for 1-2 seconds on each side.

Remove them with a slotted spoon and let them cool.

In another pot, sauté the onions and olive oil for 5 minutes.

Add all of the spices, salt, pepper, 2 cups of hot water and rice.

Let the rice boil and become soft.

When the rice is almost cooked, add the lemon juice. Leave it for a little more time into the pot and remove the pot from the heat.

Take a leaf, put a teaspoonful of the filling into the centre and wrap very tightly in little rolls.

place them by cheek and jowl in order for them to stay in place while cooking.

Pour half a glass of water over the rolls and cover with a plate.

Place the pot on the heat and let the rolls boil for about 8-10 minutes. Let them cool.

Serve the dolmades on a platter along with a little yoghurt, which has been previously stirred together with a little bit of sweet paprika.

Ingredients

50-60 small and tender grape leaves,

1 teacup of round grain rice (such as risotto or paella rice),

3 grated onions,

8-10 finely chopped spring onions,

1 bunch of finely chopped dill,

1 bunch of finely chopped fennel,

1 bunch of finely chopped parsley,

1 wine glass of olive oil,

1 water glass of lemon juice,

salt and pepper,

a little yoghurt and paprika for the garnish

Bean stew with potatoes

Plain and simple... a classic, summer dish with peppers and sun-dried tomatoes that make it special!

Serves ● ● ● ● ● ● 60'

Method

Peel the beans. Put the beans in a colander and wash with plenty of cold water.

Heat the oil in a pot and sauté the onions for 5-6 minutes.

Add the beans, peppers, tomatoes, sugar, salt and pepper.

Add water to the pot, so much as to cover up the beans and stir.

Leave the food to boil for 40-45 minutes.

Add the sun-dried tomatoes and parsley.

Leave the pot on the heat until the beans boil and the sauce thickens.

Secret

The alternative to red beans is white beans.

Ingredients

2kg red beans,

1 wine glass of olive oil,

3 diced onions,

2 diced green peppers,

1 diced Florina pepper,

4-5 tomatoes peeled and cut into chunks,

200g sun-dried tomatoes cut into chunks,

half a bunch of finely chopped parsley,

1 tsp sugar,

salt and freshly ground pepper

Sofrito (pan-fried veal with potatoes): the original recipe from Corfu!

A 'taste' from Corfu! Sofrito is one of the most famous and popular recipes of the island, with plenty of garlic and vinegar.

Serves ● ● ● ● ● 60′

Method

Pour oil in a pan and fry the potatoes.

Dredge the meat with flour and fry carefully on both sides.

Take care not to burn it.

In a shallow pot, spread the potatoes and add the meat, garlic, vinegar, oil, salt, pepper and water over them.

Leave the food to boil without stirring it, shake the pot a little bit to avoid sticking.

If necessary, add a little more water.

Secret

This recipe's key ingredient is vinegar. I usually add a great deal of it!

Ingredients

1 kg sliced veal (silverside),

1kg quartered potatoes,

half a wine glass of vinegar,

1 water glass of olive oil,

8 finely chopped garlic cloves,

2 glasses of water,

a little flour to fry the meat

© Nika111 | Dreamstime.com

Chicken stew with okra

A light and traditional recipe. Despite being somewhat underrated, okra still have many aficionados. Pay close attention to the secrets of their preparation!

Serves ●●●●●● 70'

Method

Trim and defuzz the okra, wash and put in a colander to drain.

Next, put them in a baking dish along with vinegar and leave it out in the sun for about half an hour.

In a pot, sauté the chicken along with the onions for 8-10 minutes.

Add the tomatoes, tomato purée, parsley, vinegar, salt and pepper.

Pour 2 glasses of water and let the chicken boil for 40-45 minutes.

In a pan, fry the okra (take care not to over fry them).

Remove them with a slotted spoon and add them into the pot where the chicken has boiled.

Leave them for about 10 minutes and remove from the heat.

Secret

You have to be careful when trimming the okra.
Trim around every conical stem and be careful not to pierce them, causing their juices to spill out.

Ingredients

1 mid-sized chicken (1200-1500g) cut into small pieces,

4 onions cut into rings,

1.5kg tomatoes peeled and cut into chunks,

half a wine glass of olive oil,

1 tsp tomato purée,

1 tbsp vinegar,

1kg small okra trimmed,

1 wine glass of vinegar,

a little olive oil to fry the okra,

3-4 finely chopped parsley sprigs,

salt, pepper

Stuffed aubergines (imam bayildi)

Once a Constantinople dish, now a Greek one. Simply put, you can't get enough of them!

Serves ● ● ● ● ● ● 60'

Method

Preheat the oven to 180 degrees.

Wash the aubergines, peel them and cut a slit lengthwise in each one of them.

Place a pan with oil on a heat and, when hot, start frying the aubergines.

Take them off one by one and leave them on a sheet of absorbent paper to drain.

Fry the potatoes slightly in unused oil.

Pour a little oil into a pan and, when hot, add the onions, garlic, salt, pepper and sugar.

Sauté briefly until browned. Keep a few tomatoes aside and add the rest along with the parsley into the pan.

Leave the sauce to thicken.

The filling is ready.

Put the aubergines one by one into a baking dish and fill them.

Spread the fried potatoes along the aubergines.

Sprinkle on some of the rusk crumbs and put a kefalograviera stick over every aubergine.

Add a little salt and pepper, the remaining tomatoes and a little oil over the potatoes.

Cook the aubergines in the oven for about 20 minutes.

Secret

An alternative to kefalograviera is mature, salty cheese.

Ingredients

10 black beauty aubergines,

10 quartered potatoes,

10 onions cut into rings,

13 tomatoes peeled and cut into chunks,

7-8 garlic cloves,

1 bunch finely of chopped parsley,

4 tbsp rusk crumbs,

10 oblong kefalograviera sticks,

1 coffee cup of olive oil,

sugar, salt and pepper,

a little oil for the pan

Hearty fasolada (bean soup) with plenty of celery and sweet Florina peppers!

A flavour 'made' in Greece! In many parts of Greece, this dish combines with olives, sausage or grilled herring.

Serves ●●●●●●●● 30'

Method

Soak the beans in water for about 12 hours.

Strain and set aside.

Pour water into a pan and bring it to the boil.

Once it starts boiling, add the beans and parboil them.

Strain and leave them drain.

Pour enough water in another pot and, when it starts boiling, add the parboiled beans, oil, tomatoes, onions, celery, carrots, peppers, tomato juice, salt, pepper and sugar.

Let the beans boil for quite a while on low heat and become soft.

Serve the fasolada hot.

Secret

Boil the beans until tender and soft.

Ingredients

500g mid-sized dried beans,

1 bunch of coarsely chopped celery,

7-8 carrots cut into rings,

5-6 onions cut into rings,

7-8 tomatoes peeled and cut into chunks,

1 water glass of tomato juice,

2-3 whole chilli peppers,

7-8 leeks cut into rings,

1 wine glass of olive oil,

sugar, salt, pepper, water

Stuffed courgettes with minced beef and avgolemono (egg-lemon sauce)

Stewed and delicious! Try them with or without mince! But, most of all, learn the secret to preventing the curdling of the egg-lemon sauce.

Serves ●●●●●●●○○ 60'

Method

Wash the courgettes very well. Slice off their edges, scoop out their flesh and cut a slit vertically in four points of them.

In a pot, add the oil along with all the onions and sauté for about 10 minutes. Add the minced beef, tomatoes and a little water. Leave the meat to boil, and when almost ready, add the rice, lemon juice, parsley, dill, salt and pepper. Stir and let the mince boil for another 10 minutes. Let the filling cool.

Fill the courgettes one by one and cover their open side with a piece of their flesh to keep their filling from falling apart. In a wide pot, add the courgettes one after the other. Spread their coarsely chopped flesh over them and add one tablespoon of oil and 1 glass of water. Place an upside-down large plate over the courgettes, cover the pot and let them boil over a low heat.

Prepare the egg-lemon sauce. Make a thick meringue by beating the egg whites with water, add the yolks without stopping the beating and, finally, the food's juice. Pour the lemon juice in and, next, put the avgolemono into the pot.

Serve hot.

Secret

When adding the avgolemono, the heat must be OFF, otherwise the sauce will curdle.

Ingredients

For the courgettes

10-15 courgettes,

4-5 grated onions,

5-6 finely chopped spring onions,

500g fresh minced meat,

2-3 juicy tomatoes peeled and cut into chunks,

300g rice,

1 wine glass of lemon juice,

1 bunch of finely chopped parsley,

1 bunch of finely chopped dill,

1 wine glass of olive of oil,

2 tbsp olive oil,

salt, pepper

For the egg-lemon sauce

2 eggs,

1 wine glass of lemon juice,

2 drops of water,

1 water glass of juice from the food

The traditional pastitsada... with cinnamon flavour

Perhaps one of the most popular recipes of Corfu. It is a dish with unique flavour and fragrances, having (deservedly) its own place of honour in every festive table!

Serves ● ● ● ● ● ● ● ● 90'

Method

Slice the meat into small pieces and sauté in a pot along with the onions, taking care not to overcook it.

Add the tomatoes, tomato juice, garlic, green pepper, salt, cayenne pepper and spices.

Pour plenty of water in the pot (about 3 glasses) and leave the meat boil for about 70-80 minutes.

Once the meat is cooked, add plenty of water to the pot. When the water starts boiling, add the pasta and let it boil slightly while stirring. Pour in the vinegar and wine and remove from the heat.

Serve the food on a platter.

Sprinkle a little grated cinnamon and plenty of grated cheese.

Eat while still warm.

Secret

An alternative to myzithra is hard, mature, salty cheese.

Ingredients

1kg veal (chuck or shank),

500g penne,

6-7 finely chopped onions,

1kg ripe tomatoes,

1 water glass of tomato juice,

2 garlic cloves,

1 whole green pepper,

1 tsp cayenne pepper,

2 cinnamon sticks,

1 tsp cloves,

1 tsp grated cinnamon,

1 wine glass of white wine,

2 tbsp vinegar,

1 water glass of olive oil,

salt and pepper,

a little grated myzithra cheese for the garnish

Stuffed meatloaves with omelette and graviera

Another version of the classic meatloaf in the oven. Make single rolls stuffed with omelette and simmer in an aromatic tomato sauce.

Serves ●●●●●●● 45'

Method

In a mixing bowl, knead the mince, bread, 2 eggs, peppermint, onions and tomatoes all together thoroughly.

Add salt and pepper.

In another bowl, beat 6 eggs and put them in a non-stick pan along with a very small amount of oil, the peppers, graviera, tomatoes, salt and pepper. Stir all together and, when cooked, let them cool.

To make the sauce, cook the oil, tomatoes, tomato juice, sugar, salt and pepper on a low heat.

Deglaze the sauce with white wine.

Prepare the rolls. Take a little bit of the mince, lay it on your hand and add a spoonful of the omelette.

Shape the mince into oval rolls and put them in the pot with the sauce.

Let the rolls cook on a low heat. When they become soft, remove from the heat.

Serve the rolls immediately either plain or with fried potatoes.

Ingredients for the sauce

1 wine glass of olive oil, 4 tomatoes peeled and cut into chunks, 1 water glass of tomato juice, 1 wine glass of white wine, a little sugar, salt and pepper.

Ingredients

For the meatloaves

1kg chicken mince,

500g bread soaked in water and thoroughly drained,

2 eggs,

1 bunch of finely chopped peppermint,

3 grated onions,

2 large tomatoes peeled and grated,

1 diced green pepper,

1 diced red pepper,

1 diced yellow pepper,

300g diced graviera,

6 eggs,

2 tomatoes peeled and cut into chunks,

salt and pepper

Bite-sized pieces of veal cooked in the pot with feta cheese and Kalamata olives

A simple recipe with some of the most essential ingredients of the Mediterranean diet: meat, cherry tomatoes, olives and Greek feta.

© Vangelis Paterakis

Serves ●●●●●●● 25'

Method

Dredge the meat with flour and fry in a pot with the oil over low heat, taking care not to overcook it.

Deglaze the meat with the wine and vinegar.

Add the shallots, cherry tomatoes, paprika, salt, pepper and a little water into the pot.

Leave the food to boil for about an hour.

Put the olives in a bowl of water for approximately half an hour.

Once the food is almost ready, add the olives and feta.

Leave the food on a low heat for another ten minutes until it re-absorbs its own juices and becomes soft.

Serve hot.

Ingredients

1.5kg veal cut into pieces,

30 shallots,

20 whole cherry tomatoes,

15 pitted black olives,

15 pitted green olives,

1 wine glass of olive oil,

500g feta cheese cut into chunks,

half a wine glass of white wine,

half wine glass of vinegar,

a little flour,

a little hot paprika,

salt and pepper

Artichokes with peas, potatoes and lots of lemon

Here is another 'pot' dish. Simple and casual!

Serves ●●●●●●  30'

Method

Peel the peas.

Cut off the stems of the artichokes.

Pull off the leaves from the hearts and remove the choke from their insides. Halve the hearts and put them in cold water with lemon juice to prevent their blackening.

Pour the oil into a pot and sauté the onions, leeks and herbs.

Add all the other ingredients into the pot and let them boil for about 20 minutes.

Ingredients

1kg fresh peas,

6-8 fresh artichokes,

1 grated onion,

5 finely chopped spring onions,

2 finely chopped leeks,

a little finely chopped dill,

a little finely chopped fennel,

4-5 quartered potatoes,

4 tomatoes,

1 water glass of tomato juice,

1 wine glass of olive oil,

half a wine glass of lemon juice,

half a tsp of sugar,

salt and pepper

© Franz Pfluegl | Dreamstime.com

Braised chicken with chilopites (Greek noodles)

Perhaps one of the most famous Greek Sunday dishes, when the whole family gathers.

Serves ●●●●●●○○ 20'

Method

Put the oil, onions and chicken pieces into a pot.

Sauté over a low heat for about 8-10 minutes.

Add the tomatoes, tomato purée, salt, pepper, sugar and 2 glasses of water.

Let the chicken boil. If necessary, add a little more water.

Boil the chilopites according to the instructions written on the packaging.

Once boiled, drain and immediately add them into the pot with the chicken.

Leave them to boil for 3-5 minutes and remove from the heat.

Serve sprinkled with grated myzithra.

Secret

An alternative to myzithra is hard, mature, salty cheese.

Ingredients

1300-1500g chicken cut into small pieces,

2 grated onions,

1 wine glass of olive oil,

1kg tomatoes peeled and cut into chunks,

1 tbsp tomato purée,

500g chilopites,

grated myzithra,

salt, pepper, sugar

The famous oven-baked lamb with lemon and oregano

A Greek flavour! The secret of this recipe lies in the baking process and the addition of lots of lemon juice. Try it on a Sunday afternoon.

Serves ● ● ● ● ● ●

 30'

Method

Preheat the oven to 180 degrees.

Wash the meat thoroughly, put it into a baking dish and season with salt, pepper and oregano.

With a sharp knife, make some small slits in several points of the meat and tuck some garlic pieces inside.

Peel and cut the potatoes. Season with salt and pepper, add oregano and scatter them all around the meat.

Drizzle the meat and potatoes with oil and lemon juice.

Add enough water, cover the baking dish with aluminium foil and put it in the oven. Leave the food to simmer.

When the food is almost ready, remove the foil and let the meat and potatoes brown.

Serve hot with a nice horiatiki (Greek) salad.

Ingredients

2kg lamb,

2kg potatoes,

1 wine glass of olive oil,

1 water glass of lemon juice,

6 garlic cloves,

oregano, salt and pepper

Giouvetsi cooked in the pot (veal stew)

What a lunch that is! Ideal for those mid-afternoon gatherings. Try adding little pieces of aubergines, courgettes and Florina peppers. A different giouvetsi... and very aromatic as well.

Serves ● ● ● ● ● ● 20'

Method

Heat the oil in a pot and add the onion, meat, courgette, aubergine, Florina pepper, sugar, salt and pepper.

Sauté for 3-4 minutes, while stirring constantly.

Add the tomatoes, tomato juice and vinegar, fill the pot with hot water so much as to barely cover the food and let it boil.

If necessary, add more water whilst cooking and keep boiling until the meat is cooked.

Pour 5-6 glasses of hot water and, once boiled, add the orzo.

Reduce the heat and stir constantly to prevent the orzo from sticking together.

Serve hot with freshly ground pepper and grated myzithra.

Secrets

1. Instead of orzo, you can use chilopites or whatever kind of pasta you have.
2. The giouvetsi can also be delicious when oven-baked.
3. My view is that it gets juicier when cooked in the pot.
4. An alternative to myzithra is hard, mature, salty cheese.

Ingredients

1.5kg veal (shank) cut into small pieces,

1 wine glass of olive oil,

1 diced onion,

1 diced courgette,

1 diced aubergine,

1 diced Florina pepper,

salt and freshly ground pepper,

a little sugar,

7-8 tomatoes peeled and cut into chunks,

1 wine glass of tomato juice,

a little vinegar,

500g thick orzo,

a little grated myzithra for the garnish

Cod bites with skordalia (garlic dip)

Who said it is difficult to make cod with garlic? Break the cod into bite-sized pieces and nobody will be able to stop eating...

Serves ● ● ● ● ●    60'

Method

Cut the cod into pieces, strip its skin off and put it in a large bowl of water to desalt it.

Leave it in the bowl for about 12 hours and make sure you change the water four to five times.

Drain it well and remove its bones.

In another bowl, mix the beer with the flour and add the sweet paprika along with a little bit of pepper.

Mix the ingredients well to make a batter.

In a pan, add the oil and, when hot, dip the cod pieces one by one in the batter and fry.

Prepare the skordalia dip separately.

Peel the garlic cloves and crush them well in a mortar until melted.

Scoop out the garlic into a mixing bowl and add the potatoes one by one by melting them and adding oil, vinegar, lemon juice, salt and pepper alternately.

The skordalia dip must become like a paste.

Serve the cod hot with a tablespoon of skordalia dip.

Ingredients

1000-1200g salted cod,

oil for the frying,

1 water glass of beer,

1 water glass & 2 tbsp self raising flour,

a little paprika,

1 garlic,

1.5kg potatoes boiled and peeled,

2.5 teacups oil,

half a teacup of vinegar,

half a teacup of lemon juice,

salt and pepper

Perch bianco (white) stew with lemon juice and potatoes

This is another of my mother's favourite recipes. The perch simmers in a pot with plenty of lemon juice and garlic, and is cooked to a turn! Try it with a glass of cool white wine.

© Vangelis Paterakis

Serves ● ● ● ● ● 40'

Method

Season the potatoes with salt and pepper and spread out in a wide pot.

Add the perch, garlic, salt, pepper and 2 glasses of water.

Place the pot on medium heat and let the food boil and become soft.

Shake the lemon juice and the oil vigorously in a shaker and dress the food.

Let it boil for about 3-4 minutes and remove from the heat.

Secrets

1. By the time you add the lemon oil in the pot, the food must be already cooked and dry of any juices.
2. If you prefer the food less zesty, add less lemon juice.
3. The pepper must be white.

Ingredients

1200-1300g perch cut into pieces,

1kg potatoes cut into rings,

6-7 finely chopped garlic cloves,

1 wine glass of olive oil,

1 water glass of lemon juice,

salt and white pepper

© Alexander Potapov | Dreamstime.com

Our grandmother's giouvarlakia (meatball soup)

The giouvarlakia is an underrated dish. This recipe is indeed the one our grandmothers used to cook; try it and find out yourselves! Secret No.1: prevent the meatballs from falling apart. Secret No.2: let them become soft in the pot.

Serves ●●●●●  40'

Method

In a mixing bowl, knead the ground beef, onions, rice, oil, parsley, eggs, grated tomatoes, salt and a bit of pepper all together.

Shape the mince into small meatballs and dredge with flour.

In a pot, pour some water and add one wine glass of the olive oil, a little salt, the coarsely chopped tomatoes and the lemon juice.

If you want, add a potato cut into small pieces as well.

Once the water starts to boil, put the meatballs one by one into the pot and let them cook until they become soft and tender.

Before the meatballs are ready, shake the pot 2-3 times to avoid burning them.

Take care not to stir the giouvarlakia or they will be trimmed.

Serve hot with a glass of cool white wine.

Ingredients

1kg ground beef,

1 teacup round grain rice,

4 grated onions,

1 coffee cup of olive oil,

1 bunch of finely chopped parsley,

2 eggs,

3 juicy tomatoes peeled and grated,

1 wine glass of olive oil,

1 wine glass of lemon juice,

2 juicy tomatoes peeled and cut into chunks,

a little flour, salt and pepper

Pork stew with leeks and celery... no further comment necessary

A delightful winter dish. And an excellent choice for our formal meals as well.

Serves ●●●●●●   50'

Method

Pour the water into a pot and boil the meat for about 30 minutes. Strain the meat and set it aside.

Boil the milk separately, add the leeks and let them boil for about ten minutes.

Strain the leeks very well.

Sauté the meat with the oil and spring onions in a pot for about ten minutes.

Deglaze with lemon juice and add salt and pepper.

Add the leeks, celery, dill, tomatoes and a little water to the pot.

Leave the food to boil and reabsorb its own juices.

Once the meat has boiled and become soft, you have to add the egg-lemon sauce.

Make a thick meringue by beating the egg whites with water, then add the yolks without stopping the beating and, finally, the food's juice.

Pour the lemon juice and, next, add the egg-lemon sauce to the pot.

Shake the pot to spread the egg-lemon sauce. Serve hot.

Secret

When adding the egg-lemon sauce, the heat must be OFF, otherwise the sauce will curdle.

Ingredients

1kg pork cut into pieces,

1 kg leeks cut into strips,

1 bunch of finely chopped spring onions,

1 bunch of finely chopped celery,

1 bunch of finely chopped dill,

1 wine glass of olive oil,

1 water glass of lemon juice,

500g milk,

2-3 whole peeled tomatoes,

2 eggs,

salt and pepper

For the egg-lemon sauce

2 eggs, 1 wine of glass of lemon juice, 2 drops of water, 1 water glass of juice from the food.

Stuffed aubergines with feta sauce

The aubergine is a favourite summer seasonal vegetable and combines ideally with feta.

Serves ●●●●●●○○  20'

Method

Preheat the oven to 160 degrees. In a pot, add the oil, onions and chicken and sauté over low heat for 10 minutes.

Add the peppermint, salt, pepper, sugar and tomato juice.

Leave the chicken to boil and reabsorb its own juices.

Cut a slit in 2-3 points of the aubergines, fry them and let them cool.

In a pot, pour in the milk and heat it up and add the semolina, while stirring continuously over low heat.

Once thick, remove the pot from the heat and let it cool.

Add the eggs one by one, salt, pepper, nutmeg and finally the feta, and stir all the ingredients together.

Fill the aubergines one by one with the mixture and place them in a baking dish one next to another, without leaving gaps.

Top each aubergine with a spoonful of the sauce and sprinkle with some rusk crumbs.

Pour a wine glass of water into the baking dish, add the tomatoes seasoned with salt and pepper and cover the baking dish with aluminium foil.

Cook for 20-25 minutes, remove the aluminium foil and put the food back into the oven for another 5 minutes to get a bit of colour.

Ingredients

10 aubergines,

500g diced chicken,

2 onions,

4-5 tomatoes cut into chunks,

1 bunch finely chopped peppermint,

1 wine glass of olive oil,

1 wine glass of tomato juice,

300g feta cut into chunks,

3 tbsp rusk crumbs,

salt, pepper, sugar,

2 water glasses of milk,

3 tbsp fine semolina,

2 eggs,

salt, pepper,

nutmeg,

some rusk crumbs

Cuttlefish stew with flavouring and orzo

Enjoy a delicious meal, cooked in the pot. An alternative way to try cuttlefish along with our glass of ouzo, beer or wine.

Serves ●●●●●●  40'

Method

Clean the cuttlefish, wash with plenty of water and drain very well.

Sauté the olive oil along with the onions (both the bulb and the spring ones) and leeks in a pot for 2-3 minutes.

Add the cuttlefish cut into rings (or whole if small) and deglaze with wine. Add the tomatoes, thyme, salt, pepper and sugar.

Stir and let the cuttlefish cook and the sauce thickens.

Boil the orzo separately. Strain and stir with 2 tablespoons of olive oil.

Add the orzo to the pot along with the sauce and cuttlefish, and shake the pot to mix the all ingredients together.

Serve with freshly ground pepper and finely chopped fennel.

Ingredients

1300-1500g cuttlefish,

2 onions cut into rings,

10-12 finely chopped spring onions,

3-4 finely chopped leeks,

3-4 tomatoes cut into chunks,

half a bunch of finely chopped fennel,

1 wine glass of olive oil,

1 wine glass of white wine,

1 packet of orzo,

a little thyme,

salt, pepper, sugar

Crispy, pan-fried meatballs

Who can resist eating a just-made, hot meatball? It is a taste we have loved since our very early childhood!

Serves ● ● ● ● ●   40'

Method

Put all the ingredients into a mixing bowl and knead well.

Make small meatballs and dredge them with flour.

In a pan, add the oil and, when hot, put the meatballs in and fry.

Accompany the meatballs with fried potatoes.

Ingredients

500g ground beef,

250g dry bread soaked in water and thoroughly drained,

1 egg,

2 grated onions,

half a bunch of finely chopped parsley,

half a bunch of finely chopped peppermint,

1 grated tomato,

1 coffee cup of olive oil,

salt, pepper, oregano,

oil for the frying and a little flour to the dredge the meatballs

© Juan Moyano | Dreamstime.com

Cauliflower yiahni (stew)

You thought the only way to cook a cauliflower is by boiling it, didn't you? Well, here's another way for you! A cauliflower can also be delicious when stewed with plenty of cinnamon.

Serves ●●●●● 40'

Method

Cut the white part of the cauliflower into florets, wash well and leave to drain.

Place a pan with a little oil on high heat and, when hot, briefly fry the cauliflower.

Put it into a wide pot.

In another pot, put 1 wine glass of olive oil, the onions, salt, pepper, sugar, cinnamon and tomatoes and let the sauce boil over a low heat.

Once the sauce is almost ready, add it to the pot with the cauliflower. Leave to boil until the sauce thickens.

Serve tepid or cold.

Ingredients

1kg cauliflower (white part only),

olive oil for the frying,

4 grated onions,

10 tomatoes peeled and cut into chunks,

1 wine glass of olive oil,

a little sugar, a little cinnamon, salt and pepper

© Dmitry Kosterev | Dreamstime.com

Oven-baked aromatic butter beans with herbs

Perhaps the most delicious butter beans you can ever taste! Aromatic, light and good to eat all year round.

Serves ● ● ● ●

 40'

Method

Put the butter beans in a bowl with plenty of water to soak (for about 10-12 hours). Boil them for 15-20 minutes.

Drain and set aside.

In a pot, sauté the oil along with all the onions and leeks for about 10 minutes.

Add salt, pepper and a little sugar.

Next, add the tomatoes, carrots and potatoes with some water.

Stir and leave the food on the heat for about 15 minutes.

Scoop out the beans into a baking dish.

Add the spinach, parsley, dill and put the food into the oven to reabsorb its own juices and become soft.

Serve hot to tepid. If you want, you can add a little bit of grated cheese.

Ingredients

500g butter beans,

1 wine glass of olive oil,

6-8 onions cut into rings,

200g finely chopped spring onions,

200g leeks cut into rings,

1kg tomatoes peeled and cut into chunks,

200g carrots cut into rings,

2-3 diced potatoes,

200g coarsely chopped spinach,

1 bunch of finely chopped parsley,

1 bunch of finely chopped dill,

salt and pepper

The classic moussaka; aromatic and light

The moussaka is a classic summer dish and a very tasty and hearty one as well.

Serves ●●●●●●●●●● 40'

Method

Fry the aubergines, courgettes and potatoes.

Put the onions into a pan along with the oil, sauté for 8-10 minutes and add the ground beef, tomatoes, salt, pepper, cinnamon and cloves.

Stir while adding the water little by little, and let it boil until it reabsorbs all of its own juices.

Stir to avoid making any lumps forming in the mince.

Pour the milk into the pan to heat it up and add the semolina while stirring continuously over low heat.

Once thick, remove the pot from the heat and let it cool.

Add the eggs one by one and, next, the salt, pepper, nutmeg and grated cheeses.

Stir well to mix all the ingredients together.

In a baking dish, spread the potatoes first, then the courgettes and, finally, the aubergines.

Lay the mince over and, finally, top with the béchamel sauce.

Sprinkle with sweet paprika.

Put the baking dish into a preheated oven at 160 degrees for 25-30 minutes.

Ingredients

4 sliced aubergines,

4 sliced courgettes,

4 sliced potatoes,

500g ground beef,

2 grated onions,

1kg tomatoes cut into chunks,

half a wine glass of olive oil,

salt, pepper, cinnamon, cloves,

2 water glasses of milk,

3 tbsp fine semolina,

2 eggs,

nutmeg,

200g various grated cheeses,

2 tbsp paprika

Chicken bites with dill and courgettes

An extremely light and aromatic dish, especially when the courgettes are seasonal.

Serves ● ● ● ● ● ● 40'

Method

In a pot over a low heat, brown the chicken along with the oil very well.

Add the courgettes, which you have fried first, salt, pepper and a little water.

Leave to boil.

Once almost ready, add the lemon juice and dill.

Let all the ingredients boil together and become soft (the get a nice, golden colour).

Serve hot with freshly ground pepper.

Ingredients

1 whole chicken (about 1.5kg) cut into small pieces,

5 courgettes cut into thick strips,

1 wine glass of olive oil,

1 water glass of lemon juice,

1 bunch of finely chopped dill,

salt and pepper,

freshly ground pepper for the garnish

© Juri Samsonov | Dreamstime.com

Pork stew with beans

It's time to try the beans and courgettes with pork!

Serves ●●●●●●● 30'

Method

In a pot over a low heat, sauté the pork along with the onions for about ten minutes.

Next, add the tomatoes, tomato juice, sugar, salt, pepper and a little water. Leave to boil for about half an hour.

Add all the red beans, courgettes, parsley, peppermint and some more water. Leave the food on low heat to boil and become soft.

Serve hot with freshly ground pepper.

Secrets

1. While the food is boiling, shake the pot carefully a few times.
2. Don't stir with a spoon as it will cause the beans and courgettes to fall apart.
3. The alternative to red beans is white beans.

Ingredients

1.5kg pork cut into small pieces,

500g red beans,

500g shelled barnounia beans (borlotti beans),

500g small courgettes,

1kg tomatoes peeled and cut into chunks,

1 water glass of tomato juice,

water,

3 grated onions,

1 bunch of finely chopped parsley,

1 bunch of finely chopped peppermint,

1 wine glass of olive oil,

a little sugar, salt and pepper,

a little freshly ground pepper for the garnish

Shrimp salad with rice; full of colours and aromatic!

The flavouring and lemon blend in a unique flavour that has lasted for years and years!

Serves ●●●●●●   40'

Method

Boil the rice according to the packet's instructions.

Strain and leave to cool.

In a large salad bowl, mix the rice, shrimps and all the other ingredients.

Vigorously shake the oil, lemon juice, mustard, salt, pepper and paprika all together in a shaker.

Dress the salad with the sauce and stir very well.

Cover the bowl with cling film and put it in the refrigerator to chill.

Before you serve the salad, stir it again.

Ingredients

2 teacups round grain rice,

800g boiled shrimps cleaned and cut into pieces,

1 bunch of finely chopped celery,

1 bunch of finely chopped rocket,

6-7 diced radishes,

2 green apples peeled and diced,

1 can of sweetcorn,

2 diced small cucumbers,

2-3 finely chopped spring onions,

1 water glass of olive oil,

half a water glass of lemon juice,

a little powdered mustard,

salt, freshly ground pepper,

a little sweet paprika

© Alexander Raths | Dreamstime.com

Bouillabaisse... fish soup

This dish takes us to an island. The simple and clean taste of a fresh Greek fish... if you want, add one or two shrimps or crayfish as well.

Serves ● ● ● ● ● ●

 45'

Method

Clean and wash the fish well.

In a pot over a low heat, add the oil, carrots, all the onions, celery and courgettes and sauté for about ten minutes.

Pour the water into the pot and, once boiled, add the fish and potatoes.

Once the fish is almost cooked, add salt, pepper, lemon juice, tomatoes and saffron.

Let the ingredients boil, add the bay leaf and leave the food on the heat for about ten minutes.

Put out the heat and serve the soup warm in a deep dish with freshly ground pepper.

Serve the fish in another platter.

If you want, debone the fish, cut it into small pieces and add them to each soup bowl.

Ingredients

1kg fish (dentex, grouper, scorpion fish or cod),

5 carrots cut into rings,

5 finely chopped onions,

5 whole mid-sized potatoes,

5 tomatoes peeled and cut into chunks,

1 large bunch of finely chopped celery,

5 small courgettes,

3 bay leaves,

1 wine glass of olive oil,

1 water glass of lemon juice,

1 pinch saffron,

10 ground black peppercorns,

salt and freshly ground pepper for the garnish

Loukoumades with yoghurt

Everyone can enjoy loukoumades, at any time of the day! Really now, how do we stop eating them once we start?

Makes   30 little loukoumades 60'

Method

In a mixing bowl, add the flour, yoghurt, olive oil, eggs, lemon and orange zests.

Mix all the ingredients very well until they become a homogeneous mixture.

Cover the bowl with a kitchen towel and leave it for 30 minutes.

Place a pan with oil on a heat and, when hot, add the mixture spoon by spoon and fry the loukoumades until they get a nice golden colour.

Sprinkle some walnuts and grated cinnamon onto a platter.

With a slotted spoon, take the loukoumades off the pan and put them on the platter.

Dress with the remaining walnuts, cinnamon and honey.

Ingredients

1 teacup yoghurt,

4 tbsp olive oil,

2 eggs,

half a teacup of self raising flour,

lemon and orange zest,

olive oil for the frying,

200g finely chopped walnuts,

1 tbsp grated cinnamon,

4-5 tbsp honey

© Alexstar | Dreamstime.com

Samali (semolina cake with syrup)

A classic syrupy sweet. Simple and unbelievably tasty!

Serves ● ● ● ● ● ● ● 65'

Method

Preheat the oven.

In a large mixing bowl, add the semolina, sugar, baking soda, mastic, water and orange juice, in which you have previously dissolved the baking powder.

Leave the ingredients unmixed and cover the bowl with a kitchen towel for about two hours.

Next, mix all the ingredients together very well until they become a homogeneous mixture.

Spread a little oil well in a baking dish.

Add the mixture into the baking dish, cut the sweet into pieces and bake in preheated oven for 45-50 minutes.

Prepare the syrup.

Take the baking dish off the oven, let it cool and then drizzle with hot syrup.

Secret

Serve plain or with a scoop of mastic ice cream!

Ingredients

1.5 teacup fine semolina,

1 teacup coarse semolina,

1.5 teacup sugar,

1 tsp baking soda,

1 tsp crushed mastic,

2 teacups orange juice,

1 tsp baking powder,

1 glass of water

For the syrup

2 glasses of water,

2 water glasses sugar,

3 tbsp lemon juice,

half a lemon

Homemade jam of 3 kinds of peaches

Fruit tastes great in the summer. Make a wonderful, homemade recipe to enjoy their taste all year round. Try a little jam with some yoghurt.

Makes   1kg jam

 60'

Method

Rinse the fruit very well, get rid of their pits and cut into chunks.

Pour half of the sugar into a pot, spread the fruit and pour the remaining sugar over them.

Place the pot on the heat and stir until the sugar melts.

With a slotted spoon, skim the jam.

Add the pelargonium and let the jam boil and thicken.

In order to figure out if the jam has thickened, you can put a thermometer into the pot and turn off the heat when it reaches 105°C.

Otherwise, take a teaspoon of the jam's syrup, pour it into a plate and, if it doesn't fall apart, then the jam is ready.

Add the lemon juice, let the jam boil for about 1-2 minutes and remove the pot from the heat. Let the jam cool and ladle it into sterilised, airtight jars.

Ingredients

1kg pitted peaches of different varieties (peaches, nectarines, peacherines),

700g sugar,

1.5 tbsp lemon juice,

2 pelargonium (rose geranium) sprigs

Vissinada (cherry juice): offer it to your guests!

Literally the perfect Greek treat!

Serves ●●●●●●●●   60'

Method

Rinse the sour cherries thoroughly and leave to drain in a colander.

With a special tool or a paperclip, remove the pits, put the cherries into a mixing bowl and crush them thoroughly to release all of their juice.

Strain the cherries and pour their juice into a pot along with the sugar and bring to the boil.

Once thickened, add the lemon/orange juice, leave to boil for 2-3 more minutes and remove from the heat.

The syrup mustn't be too thick, as it is in a sour cherry sweet.

Let the sour cherry juice cool and pour it into dry, sterilised bottles.

Serve in tall glasses of iced cold water.

Pour two fingers of sour cherry juice into each glass and fill the rest with water.

Stir the sour cherry juice with a spoon and serve.

Secrets

1. The sour cherry juice is a great match with yoghurt or ice cream.
2. Use a paperclip or a toothpick instead of a cherry pitter.

Ingredients

1kg ripe sour cherries,

900g sugar,

half a wine glass of lemon/orange juice

© Tiziano Casalta | Dreamstime.com

Eirini Togia

"Rena Tis Ftelias": 35 years of Greek, creative cuisine

Eirini Togia was born in Corfu and now lives in Athens with her family. She opened her first restaurant in 1979, at Ftelia Beach of Mykonos; a favourite place for the island's visitors and gourmets. This was followed by the Ftelia in Athens in 1985 and, for many years, the two restaurants operated simultaneously. For many years, "Rena Tis Ftelias" has stood out among the 10 best restaurants in Athens.

Rena represents Greek creative cuisine ethically and consistently, with an emphasis on the ingredients' quality and purity, the Mediterranean diet's basic ingredients (olive oil, fresh herbs and seasonal spices) as well as on the classic and traditional recipes.

Rena has been awarded numerous distinctions from European and international competitions. Among her recent distinctions:

• In 2008, she represented Greek cuisine during the "Greek Gastronomy Week", organised by GNTO in Beijing. For the sake of the event, an entire fridge was transported from Greece in order to ensure the ingredients' quality and purity!

• In the same year, she represented Greece at the "International Tourism Exhibition" in Shanghai, earning rave reviews from the organisers.

• In 2004, she won the "World's 2nd Best Female Chef" award in the international competition Gourmand Cookbook in Barcelona.

To date, Rena has revealed her secrets in numerous books, which have been published in various languages and have received European and international distinctions.

In 2008, the GNTO assigned Rena to write a book of "Mediterranean Recipes from Greece", which was released in English and Chinese!

In 2004, "Rena's Pastries and Desserts" won the "Best Desserts Book in the World" award in the Gourmand Cookbook contest in Barcelona.

In the same competition, the book "Greek Mediterranean Cuisine" earned special distinctions and was translated and published in English and German shortly after.

In recent years, Rena has been collaborating with renowned publishers and Greek producers on the recipes and secrets of Greek cuisine.

In 2013, she passed on the torch to her two daughters who opened their first restaurant. At present, she is preparing a TV show and participating in events abroad, where the Greek cuisine and tradition are presented.